EDGE BOOKS™

Video Games vs. Reality

TIME
FOR
ACTION

THE INSPIRING TRUTH BEHIND POPULAR
ADVENTURE VIDEO GAMES

BY: THOMAS KINGSLEY TROUPE

CAPSTONE PRESS
a capstone imprint

Edge Books are published by Capstone Press,
1710 Roe Crest Drive, North Mankato, Minnesota 56003
www.mycapstone.com

Library of Congress Cataloging-in-Publication Data
Names: Troupe, Thomas Kingsley, author.
Title: Time for action : the inspiring truth behind popular adventure
   video games / by Thomas Kingsley Troupe.
Description: North Mankato, Minnesota : Capstone Press, 2019. | Series:
   Edge books. Video games vs. reality | Audience: Age 8–14.
Identifiers: LCCN 2018006074 (print) | LCCN 2018006709 (ebook) |
   ISBN 9781543525793 (eBook PDF) | ISBN 9781543525717 (hardcover) |
   ISBN 9781543525755 (paperback)
Subjects: LCSH: Extinct cities—Juvenile literature. | Civilization, Ancient—
   Juvenile literature. | Extinct cities—Computer games—Juvenile literature. |
   Civilization, Ancient—Computer games—Juvenile literature.
Classification: LCC CC176 (ebook) | LCC CC176 .T76 2019 (print) |
   DDC 930.1—dc23
LC record available at https://lccn.loc.gov/2018006074

Editorial Credits
Aaron Sautter, editor; Kyle Grenz, designer; Tracy Cummins, media researcher;
   Tori Abraham, production specialist

Photo Credits
Alamy: JHPhoto, 17; Bridgeman Images: Embleton, Ron (1930-88)/Private
Collection/©Look and Learn, 8, Private Collection/©Look and Learn, 16; Getty
Images: Chesnot, 19, Patrick McMullan, 21; Newscom: Handout/MCT, 9, MPI
EVA Leipzig/UPI, 13; Reuters: Mike Blake, 25; Science Source: Christian Jegou
Publiphoto Diffusion, 12; Square Enix Ltd: Rise of the Tomb Raider © 2015
Square Enix Ltd. All rights reserved. RISE OF THE TOMB RAIDER, TOMB
RAIDER, and LARA CROFT are registered trademarks or trademarks of Square
Enix Ltd. SQUARE ENIX is a registered trademark or trademark of Square Enix
Holding, 10; Shutterstock: camilkuo, 29, CreativeCore, Design Element, DnDavis,
23, Evannovostro, 4, Guenter Albers, 18, Lukasz Szwaj, Design Element, Mauro
Rodrigues, Cover Middle, Ropak Tetiana, Design Element, SasinTipchai, 22,
Serhiy Smirnov, Design Element, Skreidzeleu, 14–15, theskaman306, 24, Tinxi,
27, Tish11, Design Element, vlastas, 20, weltreisendertj, 6–7; SuperStock: A.
Burkatovski/ Fine Art Images, 11; Thinkstock: digitalimagination, 26

Printed and bound in the United States of America.
PA017

TABLE OF CONTENTS

CHAPTER 1

Ready for Action!

Stone grinds against stone as the massive door slides open. The ancient temple shudders as the door comes to a stop. You gaze into the dark passage. A tattered curtain of cobwebs sways in the wind. You flick on your flashlight and take a few cautious steps inside. The shadows of ancient sculptures dance in the light as you breathe in the musty air. No one has set foot in this place for a very long time.

You hear a rumbling sound as the ceiling above you trembles. You dive out of the way as a giant block of stone slams down where you just stood. You turn to see that your only exit has been sealed off, blocked with rubble.

Suddenly, torches hanging along the passage light themselves. Some ancient magic is welcoming you to the temple. A giant **brazier** ignites, casting a fiery light into every corner of the room. Beyond it a dusty skeleton stands propped against a large stone altar. In its bony hands rests the Amulet of Life. You step forward and the ground begins to disappear beneath you. With only a second to react, you leap. You manage to catch the edge of the altar and hang on for dear life. You aren't about to die here. The **artifact** is almost within your grasp!

brazier—a metal container used to hold live coals or fuel to heat or light a room

artifact—an object used in the past that was made by people

Did you manage to get the treasure? If not, don't worry. In action-adventure video games, you'll always get another chance. Video games with ancient artifacts and daring adventurers have thrilled gamers for years. Adventure games offer travel to exotic locations and death-defying action.

Believe it or not, many elements in action-adventure video games are inspired by real-life history and places. Game creators study old **cultures** and legends to bring a sense of real history into their action titles. They research lost cities, towering pyramids, and other mysterious places to bring game settings to life. They also study **archaeology** and history. They use all of it to create incredible artifacts and challenging puzzles for heroes to solve. Grab your flashlight and some rope. It's time to explore the real inspiration behind the most popular action games.

culture—a people's way of life, ideas, customs, and traditions

archaeology—the study of historic or prehistoric cultures by examining ancient artifacts, buildings, and other things that people left behind

CHAPTER 2

Historic Inspiration

Gamers love the thrill of adventure games. But the most popular action-adventure games usually tell a story. Games often build stories around famous people or legends. These historical hooks help pull gamers into the story.

FACT

Sir Francis Drake was so hated by the Spanish, they offered 20,000 ducats for his head. Today that reward would equal more than $3 million.

Game company Naughty Dog has given gamers many exciting thrills with the cinematic adventures of Nathan Drake and his friends in the Uncharted series.

A Family Tradition

Born in 1540, Sir Francis Drake was a successful sailor and **navigator**. During his travels, Drake also led raids against Spanish ships and towns to steal their riches. The Spanish considered him to be a pirate and put a **bounty** on his head.

In *Uncharted: Drake's Fortune*, Nathan Drake believes that he's a descendant of Sir Francis Drake. During the game Nate tries to find Drake's final resting place. He thinks he'll find clues that will lead him to Drake's hidden treasure. The real remains of Sir Francis Drake have never been found. But in the game Nate does find Drake's coffin. A journal within holds clues that leads Nate on a global treasure hunt.

navigator—someone who uses maps, compasses, and the stars to travel the seas by ship

bounty—money offered for capturing a criminal

Tombs to Treasure

Some action games are linked to legendary locations. **Folklore** and myths from real cultures fuel many video game stories. Gamers experience history in a whole new way.

According to Russian folktales, the mythical city of Kitezh lies hidden deep below the surface of Lake Svetloyar. Mongol armies invaded Russia in 1238. Their leader, Batu Khan, was determined to find the lost city. He tortured people until someone told him the location. When Khan and his army arrived, they found Kitezh undefended. The people there only prayed for God to save their city. According to the legend, hundreds of fountains of water suddenly shot out of the ground. Kitezh disappeared beneath the waters of Lake Svetloyar.

folklore—tales, sayings, and customs among a group of people

In *Rise of the Tomb Raider*, gamers play the role of Lara Croft. She seeks the tomb of the Prophet. The tomb holds clues to the location of Kitezh. During her adventure Lara uncovers several clues, artifacts, and documents. They tell the tale of the Prophet and his search for the city of Kitezh. By using the actual legends of Kitezh, gamers feel as if they are part of a real quest.

FACT

As a mythical underwater city, Kitezh is sometimes known as the Russian Atlantis. Stories say that the lost city can still be seen under Lake Svetloyar. But only those who are holy and pure of heart can find it.

Stone Age Survival

Not all adventure games focus on hunting for treasure or lost cities. Some game designers like to dig even deeper into history. What would an adventure in a land before time look like?

Not much is known about how ancient cavemen and women lived. Archaeologists have studied ancient bones, cave drawings, and tools to learn more about **prehistoric** people. Researchers believe that Stone Age people were the first to use tools made of carved or chipped stone.

prehistoric—belonging to a time before history was written down

Far Cry: Primal expands on what archaeologists know. In the game, hunting for food is the most important activity for prehistoric people. Players become the character of Takkar. He collects animal skins, meat, and bones to provide for his people. He uses pieces of bone and stone to make useful hunting tools. Game designers added cave paintings to the game setting for extra realism. They even included an "ice age" region on the game map to help the world seem more realistic.

FACT

Some of the oldest human bones ever found were in the country of Morocco. Scientists believe they are about 300,000 years old.

CHAPTER 3

Lost Legends

When adventure game heroes aren't hunting for treasure, they're usually looking for lost cities. Many games use legendary lost **civilizations** as their settings.

Ancient and Abandoned

Shambhala is a mythical kingdom mentioned in ancient texts from Asia. According to legend it was a paradise. Only the pure of heart could live there. Shambhala was a land of peace where people are never hurt and never grow old. Explorers have searched for this holy land for hundreds of years. A few have claimed to find Shambhala. But no one has ever proven their findings.

civilization—a developed and organized society

Nathan Drake is on another major quest in *Uncharted 2: Among Thieves*. This time he's looking for the fabled city of Shambhala. Game designers used the adventures of famous explorer Marco Polo as inspiration for the game. Gamers follow clues left behind by Polo. Drake and his companions find their way to Tibet and the Himalayan Mountains. Eventually, they discover the legendary lost city of Shambhala.

Under the Sea

About 71 percent of the Earth is covered
in water. It makes sense that lost cities could
be beneath the sea. Using ancient legends as
inspiration, some gaming adventures have
taken place in lost underwater cities.

Perhaps the most famous of all lost kingdoms is the underwater city of Atlantis. More than 2,000 years ago, Greek philosopher Plato wrote about the city of Atlantis. He described it as a beautiful city with gold and silver statues. Plato also wrote about how the gods destroyed the city and caused the island to sink beneath the sea.

Inspired by the legend of Atlantis, game designers created *Bioshock*. The story takes place in 1960 in a ruined, underwater city called Rapture. In the game's world, the city was supposed to be a place for wealthy and famous people to live. But just like Atlantis, the underwater paradise is destroyed. Only ruins are left deep below the ocean's surface.

FACT

Bioshock was a very popular game that continued with two sequels. The latest game, *Bioshock: Infinite* takes place in an airborne city called Columbia.

Before Being Buried

Imagine exploring a busy, thriving city long before it becomes lost to time. Using archaeological research, game designers can give players a glimpse of life in these ancient cities.

Ancient Egypt may be the most famous of all ancient civilizations. Mighty Pharaohs ruled there from 3150 to 30 BC. The Pharaohs acted like they were gods, conquering and enslaving people. Using slave labor, the Egyptians built busy cities full of large statues, temples, and pyramids. The huge Pyramids at Giza were built as monuments and tombs for the Pharaohs. Today they are considered one of the Seven Wonders of the World.

FACT

Researchers think it took 20 years and 100,000 slaves to build the Great Pyramid in Egypt. It was built with about 2.3 million blocks of stone, each weighing about 2.5 tons (2.2 metric tons).

In *Assassin's Creed Origins* players are free to explore the lands of ancient Egypt as they work to carry out their missions.

In *Assassin's Creed: Origins*, players get to see what life in ancient Egypt might have been like. As the main character of Bayek, players can climb and explore temples, city squares, and statues. Players also meet famous historical figures such as Cleopatra. She ruled the Ptolemaic Kingdom of Egypt from 51 to 12 BC.

CHAPTER 4

Fortune and Glory

In most action-adventure games, there's usually one big reason why heroes risk their lives—treasure! Game creators again look to history to inspire the loot hidden in their games.

A Big Stick

Game characters are often looking to strike it rich with rare artifacts. But some items also come with the promise of power. According to the Biblical story, God chose Moses to lead the Israelites out of slavery in Egypt. God performed a number of miracles through Moses' staff. It turned into a snake in front of the Pharaoh. It also brought several plagues to the land, forcing the king to free the Israelites.

FACT

The Bible claims that Moses' staff was capable of all sorts of things. When the Israelites were thirsty, Moses struck a rock with the staff and water poured from it. When they were trapped by Pharaoh's army, Moses used the staff to part the Red Sea, allowing the Israelites to escape.

The game *Indiana Jones and the Staff of Kings* stars famous adventurer Dr. Indiana Jones. He's looking for the powerful Staff of Moses. Indy's quest leads him to countries around the world, including Panama, Nepal, and Turkey. Once he finds the staff, Indy uses it to control water and bring doom to his enemies. At one point in the game, the staff even becomes a serpent and slithers away.

Dragon Dagger

Dragons appear in legends from cultures around the world. In China these mythical beasts are especially important. In the city of Xi'an is a well-known landmark called the Blue Dragon Temple.

Chinese dragons were often believed to have magical abilities and were symbols of power for China's emperors.

In *Tomb Raider II* Lara Croft seeks out a treasure known as the Dagger of Xian. The legendary blade has incredible power. The dagger gives the holder the abilities of a fire-breathing dragon. Game designers made up the fantastic powers of the dagger. However, they based the weapon's design heavily on Chinese culture. The dagger's handle has rich golden detailing, with the blade emerging from a dragon's mouth.

FACT

In Hindu mythology Ganesh is known as the Lord of Good Fortune and the Remover of Obstacles.

A Treasured Tusk

One of the most worshipped **deities** of the Hindu people is Ganesh. He is often represented with an elephant's head that is missing one tusk. In Hindu legends, Ganesh guarded his father, Lord Shiva, while he slept. A Brahmin warrior named Parashurama wanted to see Shiva but Ganesh wouldn't let him pass. Parashurama rushed at Ganesh in anger. Ganesh could have easily defeated him. But he knew that Parashurama's axe was a gift from Lord Shiva. Rather than bring shame to his father, Ganesh allowed his left tusk to be cut off.

deity—a god or a goddess

The Tusk of Ganesh is the artifact sought by the heroes in *Uncharted: The Lost Legacy.* The game reflects the history of Ganesh and his encounter with Parashurama. Game designers added jewels and fine metals to the tusk to make it a valuable treasure. The game makers also sprinkled details from the old story into the game. For example, images and figures of Parashurama's axe and Ganesh's tusk are used to solve several puzzles in the game. Game designers hoped adding these details would add a touch of realism.

V In *Uncharted: The Lost Legacy*, gamers follow several clues based on Indian mythology to find the lost treasure.

Apple of Eden's Eye

One highly-prized game treasure is based on another Biblical story. The story says that God created Adam and Eve to be the very first people on Earth. God created a beautiful garden, called Eden, for them to live in. They were given one simple rule to follow—don't eat fruit from the Tree of Knowledge. But Adam and Eve disobeyed and ate the fruit anyway. God then **banished** them from Eden.

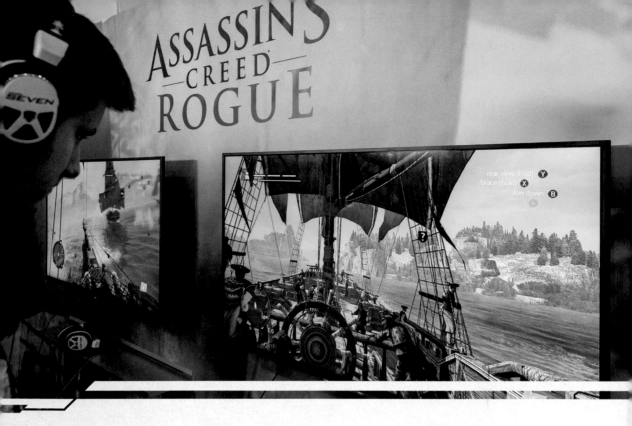

In the Assassin's Creed series, players look for a **mystical** artifact known as the Apple of Eden. It isn't a piece of fruit, but game makers were inspired by the legend. In the game, the Apple of Eden can be combined with other pieces from Eden. Whoever has the Eden artifacts can control people's minds—and the world.

FACT

The Assassin's Creed games are filled with characters based on real-life historical figures. Benjamin Franklin, Leonardo DaVinci, and the feared pirate Blackbeard are a few of the famous people who have appeared in the series.

banish—to send away forever

mystical—relating to having supernatural qualities or abilities

Adventure Awaits!

From exploring lost cities to finding valuable treasure, game makers work hard to keep players excited. Grand adventures around the world and intense action are just some of the appeal. The amazing part is knowing that these games are based on real people and legends from history.

Gamers love to become **virtual** heroes in action-packed stories. Grounding a story in history lets players build the adventure from a familiar start. Adventure games are often exaggerated with wild action and even supernatural elements. But small historical details can add flavor to the fun. Basing a game on real life helps broaden gamers' sense of the world. As they dodge bullets, solve puzzles, and hunt for amazing treasures, players can learn a little real-world history.

virtual—not real; when something is made to look real on a computer

GLOSSARY

archaeology (ar-kee-OL-uh-jee)—the study of historic or prehistoric cultures by examining ancient artifacts, buildings, and other things that people left behind

artifact (AR-tuh-fakt)—an object used in the past that was made by people

banish (BAN-ish)—to send away forever

bounty (BAUN-tee)—money offered for capturing a criminal

brazier (BRAY-zher)—a metal container used to hold live coals or fuel to heat or light a room

civilization (si-vuh-lih-ZAY-shuhn)—a developed and organized society

culture (KUHL-chuhr)—a people's way of life, ideas, customs, and traditions

deity (DEE-uh-tee)—a god or a goddess

folklore (FOHLK-lohr)—tales, sayings, and customs among a group of people

mystical (MIS-ti-kuhl)—relating to having supernatural qualities or abilities

navigator (NAV-uh-gay-tuhr)—someone who uses maps, compasses, and the stars to travel the seas by ship

prehistoric (pree-hi-STOR-ik)—belonging to a time before history was written down

virtual (VIR-choo-uhl)—not real; when something is made to look real on a computer

READ MORE

Barber, Nicola. *Lost Cities.* Treasure Hunters. Chicago: Capstone Raintree, 2013.

Capek, Michael. *Unsolved Archaeological Mysteries.* Unsolved Mystery Files. North Mankato, Minn.: Capstone Press, 2016.

Fullman, Joseph. *Ancient Civilizations.* DK Eyewitness Books. New York: DK Publishing, 2013.

INTERNET SITES

Use FactHound to find Internet sites related to this book.

Visit *www.facthound.com*

Just type in 9781543525717 and go.

 Check out projects, games and lots more at **www.capstonekids.com**

INDEX